THE VOL. 2 SUPER COLOSSAL BOOK OF HIDDEN PICTURES

Compiled by the Editors of Highlights for Children

MORE THAN 2,200 OBJECTS TO FIND

BACKPACKBOOKS
o
NEW YORK

By the Stream

As the catfish swim lazily downstream, try to find these hidden objects: a banana, hairbrush, screwdriver, teacup, spoon, mushroom, watering can, bowl, book, ice-cream cone, toothbrush, domino, and a wishbone.

This edition published by Barnes & Noble, Inc.
by arrangement with Boyds Mills Press. Inc.
Printed in the United States of America

U.S. Cataloging-in-Publication Data
(Library of Congress Standards)

The super colossal book of hidden pictures, volume 2 / compiled by
the editors of Highlights for Children.—1st ed.
[192] p. : ill. ; cm.
Summary: Each page presents a challenge to find various objects
within an illustration.
ISBN 0-7607-4875-6
1. Picture puzzles. I. Highlights for Children. II. Title.
793.73 21   2001   AC   CIP

First Barnes & Noble edition, 2003
The text of this book is set in 10-point Clarendon Light.

10 9 8 7 6 5 4 3

Basketball Fun

The score is tied. Who will score the next basket? While the teams go for the ball, you can go for thirteen hidden objects in the gym. Look for a ring, banana, tube of toothpaste, rabbit, pencil, butter knife, shovel, slice of pie, baseball bat, horseshoe, sailboat, slice of bread, and a wristwatch.

3

Return from the Sea

These voyagers are so happy to be home that they don't notice they've brought fifteen hidden objects with them. Find a bird, stork, two kangaroos, iron, key, two cats, bell, guitar, rabbit, teacup, sock, belt, and a sea gull.

Spot's Bath

The children have their hands full trying to give Spot a bath. See if you can spot twenty-four hidden objects in this soapy scene. Find a ghost, sock, bell, wedge of cheese, pear, crescent moon, telescope, heart, mushroom, tack, penguin, paintbrush, lollipop, ladle, mug, turtle, broccoli, ring, sailboat, ax, crayon, cupcake, ice-cream pop, and a bat.

5

Make a Wish

It's Rachel's birthday and the candles are lit. While the birthday girl tries to blow out all nine of them, see if you can find the fourteen hidden objects in the backyard. Look for a turtle, baseball bat, saltshaker, pumpkin, fish, boomerang, bowling ball, envelope, snake, hairbrush, tube of paint, mushroom, needle, and a book.

Sack Race

Who will win the race? While the children hop to the finish line, race to find a fishhook, teacup, slipper, hat, banana, bell, toothbrush, worm, hockey stick, candy, slice of watermelon, and a spoon.

Rabbit Colony

The rabbits and their neighbors are doing chores and having fun. Join in by searching for thirty-one hidden objects. Dig for a duck, scarf, clarinet, yo-yo, balloon, hoe, grasshopper, butterfly, safety pin,

bell, coffeepot, envelope, fish, trowel, saw, cupcake, belt, hammer, crescent moon, key, snake, snail, eyeglasses, frog, candy cane, hockey stick, fishhook, ring, bottle, ladle, and a comb.

Mom and Baby Dinosaur

It's lunchtime and the dinosaurs are searching for juicy green leaves. While they munch, you can search for a hat, artist's brush, fish, tweezers, scissors, bowling ball, safety pin, bird, bell, acorn, cherries, bee, needle, and a banana.

Sleds and Snowmen

There's no school today, and the children are having fun in the snow. While they do, look for a candle, slice of cake, needle, key, sneaker, paintbrush, slice of pie, bell, spoon, cupcake, pushpin, and a wishbone.

Clean-up Time

Leah and Justin are washing up before bedtime and don't notice the twelve hidden objects around them. See if you can find a pennant, worm, hoe, lollipop, wooden shoe, banana, golf club, drumstick, slice of cake, top hat, fish, and a paintbrush.

Busy Chipmunks

It's time to store nuts for the coming winter months, and the chipmunks are doing just that. While they scurry around, see how quickly you can find a hat, pencil, egg, toothbrush, carrot, spoon, saw, duck, horn, bell, tweezers, paper clip, and a fish.

Surf's Up!

These two windsurfing dogs are having a ball battling the waves. Before they wipe out, see if you can find thirteen hidden objects. Look for a kite, duck, pennant, fish, top hat, horn, sailboat, hammer, gopher, ice-cream cone, baseball bat, frog, and a banana.

Trick-or-treaters

What goodies can the children find in the castle? While they go for treats, treat yourself and find a broom, sock, trowel, crescent moon, candle, cat, shoe, witch's hat, fire hydrant, frying pan, pliers, baby's bottle, toothbrush, bird, and a book.

Birdhouse Builders

Josh and Dustin are so busy building their birdhouses that they don't see the twelve hidden objects around them. See if you can find a fish, open book, comb, lollipop, crescent moon, slice of watermelon, toothbrush, tack, ladle, teacup, banana, and a pencil.

Morning Crows

While the crows get an early start to their day, see if you are awake enough to find a comb, fish, shoe, fishhook, rabbit, snake, cat, glove, heart, slice of bread, paper clip, pitchfork, and a spoon.

Kitty Cat Acrobats

The circus starts tomorrow, and these cats are trying to get their act together. While they practice, search the scene for a whistle, rabbit, rolling pin, crown, glove, hammer, teacup, dolphin, wristwatch, cupcake, hat, handbell, and a butterfly.

A Ride in the Woods

Kirsten and Cory are enjoying the beauty of the forest and don't see the thirteen hidden objects around them. Help them find a rabbit, mouse, banana, pennant, frying pan, bowl, saltshaker, shovel, needle, bird, hairbrush, fishing pole, and a squirrel.

Cat at the Bird Feeder

Tabby is in the neighborhood, and the birds are taking off. While this frisky feline hangs on, see if you can find a spatula, eyeglasses, fish, artist's brush, bicycle pump, pencil, mallet, crayon, pushpin, safety pin, spoon, and a musical note.

20

Building a Bigger Soddy

There's work to be done, and Rover isn't helping! While the family tries to get him off the roof, see if you can discover a chair, hairbrush, tepee, shark, C-clamp, pencil, ax, screwdriver, mug of coffee, teddy bear, book, bird, toolbox, and a light bulb.

Belling the Cat

Shhh! Fluffy is sound asleep and doesn't know what the mice are up to. There are mice everywhere!

See if you can find forty-four of them before he wakes up.

Friendly Neighborhood

The people in this neighborhood don't know that there are thirteen hidden objects around them. Find a pencil, slice of pie, screwdriver, nail, ice-cream pop, toothbrush, lollipop, shoe, envelope, boot, kite, handbell, and a candle.

Night Music

The lizards are enjoying this nighttime serenade in the forest. While they dance to the music, search for a seal, pennant, duck, mouse, suitcase, stork, dragonfly, sailboat, scissors, hairbrush, fork, insect, bow tie, and a spoon.

25

First Snow

The children are getting ready to go out and play in the snow. You can get ready to find thirteen hidden objects. Can you spot a book, pencil, heart, dog, flag, paintbrush, candle, sneaker, light bulb, caterpillar, snail, chicken, and a banana?

The Seamstress

There is lots going on in this busy shop. Search for a shoe, pear, cookie, nail, hair dryer, ruler, penguin, pitcher, elephant, ladle, ear of corn, hat, straight pin, ice scraper, and a banana.

Amelia Earhart

While the excited fans wait for the famous pilot's autograph, see if you can find a squirrel, broom, sock, baseball bat, seal, hammer, fan, snail, key, canoe, thimble, butterfly, mushroom, pencil, high-heeled boot, and a handbell.

The City Mouse and the Country Mouse

Reginald and his cousin Jethro are enjoying a feast, but there's trouble below! Maybe one of the fourteen hidden objects will help distract the cat. Search for a key, banana, book, eyeglasses, fish, ring, megaphone, ladder, hanger, pair of pants, eagle's head, paper clip, comb, and a duck.

Hide-and-Seek

Amanda knows the other children are hiding, but she doesn't know about the twelve objects hiding as well. Help her find a rabbit, saltshaker, fish, trowel, slice of pizza, spoon, pencil, sock, crescent moon, open book, hammer, and a bird.

High-Flying Mice

The Mouse brothers are airborne over the countryside in search of hidden objects. Do you think they'll find a carrot, book, mitten, pushpin, spatula, radish, wishbone, nail, slice of pie, ice-cream cone, candle, and a hoe?

The Icing on the Cake

The baker is so busy putting the finishing touches on his masterpiece that he doesn't see thirteen hidden objects in his bakery. Find a ring, comb, drinking straw, snake, boot, hat, telephone receiver, artist's brush, fishhook, golf club, tack, eyeglasses, and a banana.

32

Out for a Stroll

Mama Ostrich is taking her babies for a walk along the shore. She doesn't know there are fourteen hidden objects here. Can you find a mouse, flashlight, sock, magnifying glass, fish, hairbrush, frog, anchor, pitcher, rabbit, light bulb, carrot, lizard, and a candle?

Hit the Ice!

The players are getting ready for the big hockey game and don't see the twenty-five hidden objects in the locker room. Look for an open book, sock, tube of toothpaste, ax, flowerpot, baseball cap, butterfly, mug, apple, banana, slice of bread, ice-cream cone, bell, wishbone, mouse, mushroom, mallet, cupcake, magnifying glass, pennant, pitcher, egg, pencil, saucepan, and a needle.

Biking Together

It's a great day for a bike ride and a picnic in the park. Along the trail, spot the cane, bell, alligator, dinosaur, pencil, iron, paintbrush, fish, soda can, balloon, paper airplane, bottle, toothbrush, computer screen, and two dogs' heads.

On Safari

There's lots to see on this safari, including twenty-six hidden objects. See if you can find a boot, spoon, safety pin, frying pan, ice-cream cone, flag, teacup, book, toothbrush, fish, ring, comb, heart, duck,

hat, T-shirt, gingerbread man, cat, tweezers, kite, crown, tack, glove, bell, paper clip, and a pitchfork.

Aquarium Fun

Andrew is watching over his favorite fish. You can look for a saltshaker, crayon, scissors, open book, knitted cap, spoon, mushroom, shovel, rabbit, worm, seal, sneaker, and a cupcake.

Sculpting

Kristen is concentrating on her sculpture of her sister and doesn't notice the hidden objects in the studio. Can you find a pear, eyeglasses, wooden shoe, rowboat, teacup, spool of thread, penguin, fishhook, brick, peanut, banana, baseball bat, and a feather?

Box Turtles

These two turtles are surrounded by thirteen hidden objects. Search the pond for a top hat, rooster, mouse's head, hand mirror, bow tie, artist's brush, ax, hourglass, slice of bread, butter knife, ice-cream cone, needle, and a knitted cap.

Pajama Party

The girls are having fun together, even though they're surrounded by hidden objects. Find a mitten, spoon, ice-cream cone, lollipop, slice of pie, turtle, question mark, pennant, crayon, knitted cap, snake, slice of cake, mushroom, fish, artist's brush, tube of toothpaste, sailboat, bell, bird, birdhouse, tack, trowel, open book, and a drinking glass.

On the Trail

Three little kittens have lost their way. While they search for the right path, you can search for a cherry, acorn, mouse, carrot, turtle, chicken, rabbit's head, teacup, snail, bee, bird, crab, number 7, paper clip, needle, and a fish.

Fishing with Dad

Who will catch the biggest fish? Who will find all the hidden objects? Look for a mug, shovel, pliers, radish, toothbrush, ballpoint pen, nail, fish, spoon, artist's brush, musical note, eyeglasses, and a fishhook.

Chanticleer

While Chanticleer wakes everyone up, search for a snail, plate, ruler, rabbit, seal, sailboat, toothbrush, butterfly, dog, dolphin, mouse, paper clip, teacup, key, fish, and a banana.

Jump Ball

Which team will win? You'll be a winner if you can find a bowl, seal, cat, golf club, baseball cap, sailboat, worm, teapot, banana, fish, pitcher, carrot, and a teacup.

Seesaw Fun

Mama Elephant is happy to see her twins having such a good time. While they play, see if you can find twenty-five hidden objects in the park. Look for a snake, handbell, horn, closed umbrella,

46

horseshoe, ladle, dragonfly, bowl, flaming torch, trowel, fork, scissors, crown, boomerang, flag, cane, cherry, pencil, button, light bulb, needle, fish, crescent moon, ice-cream cone, and a yo-yo.

Little Big Rig

While Josh hauls Sandy around the neighborhood, see if you can find a baseball cap, teacup, horn, ice-cream cone, toothbrush, fish, needle, banana, crown, flag, feather, heart, paper clip, slipper, and a pencil.

48

The Shoe Boat Sets Sail

The mice are off in search of new sights. See what sights you can find in this scene. Search for a paper clip, pennant, dragonfly, high-heeled shoe, bow tie, iron, mug, telephone receiver, bird, key, saw, elf's hat, spoon, and a centipede.

Up a Tree

The children are set for a relaxing afternoon in the tree. They don't notice the twelve hidden objects up there with them. Can you find a bowl, crescent moon, slice of pizza, teacup, banana, butterfly, slice of lemon, toothbrush, apple core, spoon, fork, and an artist's brush?

County Fair

Have some fun at the fair while you search for a cupcake, crown, baseball cap, goose, hatchet, toothbrush, fish, ladder, ice-cream cone, carrot, butterfly, ice-cream pop, handbell, artist's brush, and a pencil.

Fright Night

Scout and Mittens are enjoying their favorite scary movie. Don't be afraid to look for a heart, pennant, ice-cream cone, sheep, fish, hand mirror, trowel, letter *V*, cane, ladder, letter *U*, bee, arrow, letter *L*, letter *F*, cat's head, artist's brush, and a bird.

Pirate Treasure

The children have discovered Sparky's hidden treasure. See if you can discover thirteen objects that are still hidden in this scene. Find a bird, dinosaur, banana, sailboat, ladder, ice-cream pop, heart, baseball bat, shoe, comb, pennant, football, and a mitten.

Hoteiosho Comes to the Santa Claus Party

These Japanese children are having lots of fun waiting for Hoteiosho to arrive. While they celebrate, see if you can find a tack, banana, jack-o'-lantern, bird, worm, baseball, ram's head, hot-air balloon, deer's head, duck, telescope, ruler, insect, and a battery.

The Grasshopper and the Ants

Who will be ready for winter? Before the snow flies, see if you can find a saw, top hat, eagle's head, plate, glove, pencil, hammer, flag, megaphone, alligator, nail, artist's brush, fish, and a crown.

Pumpkins for Sale

There are so many interesting faces to choose from, Jordan doesn't see the sixteen hidden objects all around him. Can you find a sailboat, bird, mushroom, crescent moon, question mark, tepee, fish, pitchfork, needle, cat, lollipop, pliers, banana, umbrella, rabbit's head, and a tack?

Making a Snowman

While Josiah and Amber put the finishing touches on their snowman, see if you can find a drumstick, apple, sock, mitten, bell, dog, elf, heart, elf's hat, ice skate, candle, squirrel, slice of cake, snowmobile, ice-cream cone, crayon, and a knitted cap.

57

Ye Merry Travelers

The villagers are about to be entertained by this merry troupe of performers. Entertain yourself by finding a shovel, tack, arrow, rabbit's head, crescent moon, teacup, spatula, trowel, envelope, pickax,

telephone pole, sailboat, eyeglasses, ladle, fish, mushroom, chicken, hanger, hoe, stork's head, banana, slice of pizza, fishing pole, candle, boomerang, ladder, needle, frying pan, closed umbrella, and a domino.

Dinner Is Served

Mr. Rooster is so hungry that he doesn't see twelve hidden objects in the restaurant. Can you find a chair, doll, bottle, boot, hourglass, fan, octopus, pacifier, fish, horse, jester's head, and a banana?

Victory!

The home team has just won the opening game and the celebration is on! While the team enjoys the victory, see if you can find a sheep, mushroom, wedge of cheese, artist's brush, starfish, dog bone, radish, three arrows, slice of pie, hedgehog, slice of bread, and a worm.

Flying Kites

While the kids see how long they can keep their kite flying, fly around this scene and find a pennant, spoon, key, portable radio, rabbit, ice-cream cone, saltshaker, fish, slice of pie, bat, pear, artist's brush, knitted cap, tack, and a lollipop.

Mother Goose

Mother Goose is busy making sure all the geese get fed. Can you spot the thirteen hidden objects around her? Look for a feather, mitten, cat, sheep, dog bone, spoon, sock, sailboat, rowboat, pencil, potato, bear, and a hanger.

Salamander Grand Prix

It's almost race time and the salamanders are scurrying to get their entry ready. Race around this scene and find a pie, baseball bat, turtle, cat, glove, three birds, potato, high-heeled shoe, butterfly, pliers, rabbit, candle, wishbone, mouse, bear cub, and a wristwatch.

Waterfall Hikers

While the kids enjoy the beauty of this scene, look for a whistle, magnifying glass, toothbrush, hammer, feather, bell, pencil, fish, hoe, chair, paintbrush, and a closed umbrella.

Tide Pool

So many interesting things are in the tide pool that the kids don't notice the twelve hidden objects all around them. Search for a hairbrush, sock, tree, ax, sailboat, mushroom, ice-cream cone, strawberry, carrot, bird, acorn, and a pencil.

By the Light of the Moon

The alligators are enjoying their moonlight canoe ride. As they paddle along, see if you can find a ring, pail, light bulb, plunger, toothbrush, mallet, closed umbrella, mug, penguin, fishhook, duck, fork, and a pencil.

Hang Ten!

Before the hidden objects get waterlogged, find a book, dog bone, penguin, Santa's hat, ice-cream pop, wishbone, fork, apple core, light bulb, artist's brush, bird, mouse, pencil, and a spoon.

The Amazing Flying Machine

While the family imagines what it would be like to take off in this contraption, imagine that you can find all fourteen hidden objects in the scene. Look for a flashlight, loaf of bread, hammer, bird, binoculars, letter *C*, nail, kite, pitcher, clarinet, violin bow, cat's head, hockey stick, and a hat.

Farm Life

It's a beautiful morning and the farm is a busy place. Keep yourself busy by trying to find forty hidden objects. Search for a dragon's head, sock, slice of pie, leaf, spoon, whale, seal, closed umbrella, two fish, two rabbits, rooster, ballpoint pen, chick, dandelion, artist's brush, squirrel, ladder, feather,

slice of bread, goose, owl, three birds, elf's head, shoe, cat, mouse, milking stool, feather duster, needle, zipper, saucepan, crescent moon, lizard, carrot, dog, and a light bulb.

Canoe Ride

As these critters head downstream in search of adventure, you can search for thirteen hidden objects. Look for a bird, comb, heart, mouse, nail, fish, goose, snake, elf's hat, crescent moon, spoon, fork, and a hammer.

Snow Time

What are the kids constructing? While they work on their creature, find a feather, candle, wishbone, hammer, recorder, shovel, magnifying glass, carrot, closed umbrella, clothespin, paintbrush, and a mug.

Bear's Birthday Party

As the Bear family celebrates Barney Bear's second birthday, find a baseball cap, comb, three birds, pennant, elf's hat, horn, car, saw, spoon, closed umbrella, nail, and a key.

Watermelon Treat

The kids are enjoying a cool, tasty treat on a hot day. Enjoy yourself as you look for a hammer, comb, carrot, fork, party hat, book, baseball cap, bird, hat, fish, banana, witch's hat, and a tack.

Hobbyhorse Roundup

The children are having so much fun pretending to be cowpokes that they don't notice twelve hidden objects around them. Can you find a bowling pin, tack, sock, teacup, handbell, candle, key, duck, fish, sneaker, snake, and a crescent moon?

Ice Skating in the Park

Lace up your skates and glide across the ice. While you do, search for a cupcake, ice-cream cone, dog's head, jump rope, pencil, slice of bread, paper airplane, soda can, rabbit, iron, hairbrush, orange, bell, and an artist's brush.

The Spider and the Fly

Will the spider catch the fly? Can you find all the hidden objects? Look for a feather, open book, sailboat, heart, spoon, fish, teacup, baseball cap, horn, ladder, straight pin, kite, crown, dog, and a mouse.

Tom Sawyer

Can Tom convince all his friends that whitewashing the fence is fun? While he tries, see if you can locate a flashlight, hummingbird, whistle, light bulb, pear, radish, teacup, safety pin, bell, book, spoon, ice-cream pop, feather, hairbrush, flower, and a toothbrush.

Lunch Break

After a busy morning on the job, these construction workers are enjoying lunch. While they take a break, look for a candle, spatula, ballpoint pen, slice of cake, book, wrench, teacup, screw, slice of pie,

padlock, crayon, ice-cream pop, whistle, key, mushroom, pencil, celery, cupcake, mallet, flower, ladle, golf club, artist's brush, shovel, and a toothbrush.

Garden Surprise

Look what Jake found in the garden! Can you find eighteen hidden objects? Search for a screw, broom, baseball bat, artist's brush, two birds, pig, carrot, ladder, knitted cap, rabbit, telephone receiver, funnel, nail, butter knife, fish, chess pawn, and a spoon.

Strange Catches

The cats aren't having much luck catching fish. See if you can fish for thirteen hidden objects. Find a fork, mallet, spoon, shark, fishhook, sock, glove, comb, rabbit, ring, butter knife, needle, and a nail.

The Animals' Golf Tournament

Buddy Beaver is hoping to get the ball in the hole with his next shot. While he concentrates, look for a pumpkin, snake, toothbrush, teacup, pencil, pliers, ring, sailboat, key, fish, coffeepot, airplane, mushroom, boot, and a bird.

Whose Bath Is It?

Scamp is escaping and Tiger's getting soaked! While Jeremy tries to get his canine under control, look for a ring, rabbit, spoon, bird, eyeglasses, needle, hammer, scissors, whistle, butterfly, ice-cream cone, and an artist's brush.

Pool Pals

The bugs are having so much fun that they don't notice fourteen hidden objects around them. Can you discover a ring, banana, fish, crescent moon, glove, crown, fishhook, heart, horn, straight pin, ruler, paper clip, toothbrush, and a teacup?

Barnstormers

These flyers have a great view of the countryside. Enjoy the sights while you look for a mitten, pliers, comb, safety pin, half an apple, book, shoe, paintbrush, pushpin, cupcake, feather, hoe, trowel, bell, radish, and a pencil.

Halloween Night

These little ghosts and goblins are out in search of treats. Treat yourself to a search for fourteen hidden objects. Look for a sock, iron, loaf of bread, clothespin, wristwatch, slice of cake, cat, flashlight, teacup, knitted cap, owl, baby's rattle, telephone receiver, and a pencil.

Sailing on the Bay

These happy sailors don't know that there are thirteen hidden objects floating around them. Find a shovel, seal, slice of cake, arrow, needle, book, carrot, wishbone, toothbrush, candle, ice-cream cone, ice scraper, and a golf club.

Oral Report

Danielle is giving her first report, and she is too nervous to notice the twelve hidden objects in the classroom. See if you can find a banana, toothbrush, artist's brush, feather, pear, bird, boomerang, sailboat, slice of pie, kite, flowerpot, and a fork.

Spring Shower

It's fun to play in the warm spring rain. Have fun while you find a dolphin, pig, heart, rhinoceros, turtle, sea horse, koala bear, bear's head, frog, lady's head, butterfly, candy cane, and a bird.

Dinosaur Swimming Hole

Do you think this is what dinosaurs did for fun? While these characters cool off, see if you can find a glove, baseball bat, sailboat, mouse, spoon, butter knife, belt, candle, mallet, bird, witch's hat, cane, and a seal.

Fourth of July Picnic

These twins are enjoying some summer picnic goodies. Enjoy yourself as you search for a lollipop, hatchet, mushroom, goblet, ring, sailboat, arrow, yo-yo, balloon, snake, top, needle, funnel and a candle.

Dinosaur Bike Ride

Mom and Baby *Triceratops* are off for a ride on their first two-wheeler. While they get some exercise, see if you can find a slice of bread, recorder, bell, carrot, butter knife, scrub brush, flashlight, mallet, half an apple, crayon, fountain pen, and a shoe.

Fire Fighter Fred to the Rescue!

Poor Frisky climbed too high and is afraid to climb back down. While she waits for help, you can help search for fourteen hidden objects. Find a carrot, sneaker, rabbit, lollipop, golf club, mug, snake, ice-cream cone, sheep, spoon, duck, cane, glove, and a telephone receiver.

Circus Wagon

The circus troupe is traveling to another town. As they roll on, find a belt, iron, squirrel, teacup, fishhook, key, pennant, hammer, spoon, toothbrush, car, pencil, horn, and a handbell.

Martins' House

These martins have just moved into a new home. While they gather seeds for dinner, you can gather thirteen hidden objects. Look for a horn, ring, needle, pencil, toothbrush, open book, glove, fish, bell, kite, comb, sock, and a saw.

Castaway Kitty

What will Kitty catch? Can you catch the hidden objects in this scene? Find a slice of watermelon, saltshaker, banana, sock, balloon, shoe, fork, crescent moon, bowling pin, magnet, doll, butterfly, vase, bowl, spoon, bird, and a comb.

TIM DAVIS

Shark Show

Sammy and Sandy Shark are all spruced up and ready to entertain the underwater world. Entertain yourself and find thirteen hidden objects in this watery scene. Find a pennant, pencil, duck, glove, chicken, ice-cream cone, sailboat, eyeglasses, saw, crescent moon, crown, camel, and a banana.

Hot Dog Stand

While these two friends grab a yummy snack, see if you can find a worm, golf club, tack, shoe, sock, heart, crown, cupcake, pencil, spoon, hammer, number 8, ring, and a drumstick.

Giraffe's Barbershop

While Lion gets a trim, see if you can find thirteen hidden objects in the shop. Look for a squirrel, hammer, handbell, screwdriver, rabbit, flashlight, artist's brush, slipper, frog, pencil, toothbrush, duck, and a penguin.

Songs Around the Campfire

Sing along with the kids around the campfire while you look for hidden objects. Can you find a pitcher, rabbit, turtle, poodle, sock, cat, goose, spoon, kite, mouse, sea gull, paintbrush, bat, and an iron?

Paper Pals

These happy desk supplies are just waiting to help with your next school project. Get creative and find a sailboat, fish, two eggs, eyeglasses, saw, toothbrush, banana, comb, crescent moon, stick of gum, roller skate, heart, and a mug.

Come to the Fair

Look at all the things to do and see at the fair. While you explore, see if you can find a book, feather, nail, carrot, grapes, mallet, hammer, butter knife, key, crayon, fountain pen, spoon, celery, toothbrush,

slice of pie, candle, pencil, bell, mitten, screwdriver, apple core, slice of cake, artist's brush, radish, and a razor.

Sculpting Mount Rushmore

While the workers put the finishing touches on George Washington's face, search for a pencil, pie, paintbrush, spoon, comb, horseshoe, golf club, pushpin, gravy boat, needle, elf's shoe, sock, squirrel, tape dispenser, and a hanger.

The Tortoise and the Hare

Look who has won the race! While the animals celebrate, find a rhinoceros, fish, eagle's head, ice-cream cone, bell, paper clip, rocking horse, crown, open book, saw, toothbrush, heart, banana, teacup, and a glove.

Reading Together

The kids are wrapped up in the exciting story, so they don't see some of their favorite *Highlights* characters and many other hidden objects all around them. Look for Goofus, Gallant, Tommy Timbertoe, Spot, Aloysius the Wolf, Poozy Bear, a closed umbrella, artist's brush, bee, ladle, apple, butterfly, baseball bat, star, needle, banana, necktie, candle, bird's head, eyeglasses, pennant, insect, and a pencil.

Bug Golf

While Connie Cricket tries to hit the ball, see if you can find thirteen hidden objects in the scene. Search for a pencil, banana, dog, shovel, eyeglasses, handbell, fish, paper clip, wild turkey, heart, toothbrush, sailboat, and an ice-cream cone.

Circus Parade

The animals are leading the way to the Big Top for today's show. As you follow along, look for a mop, toothbrush, milking stool, spoon, teacup, boot, open book, bell, hat, lollipop, balloon, crescent moon, and a hammer.

Rubbish Raider

Randy Raccoon is getting into trouble. See if you can find a golf club, screw, magnifying glass, slice of cake, spoon, mallet, ice-cream cone, tube of toothpaste, bell, artist's brush, book, and a pencil in this messy backyard.

Grandpa's Trains

Cody and Grandpa are having lots of fun with this model train set. While the train circles the track, look for a flashlight, light bulb, sailboat, ice-cream cone, two hearts, spoon, doughnut, toothbrush, dog, horn, banana, duck, book, and a pencil.

Who Jumped Over the Moon?

After you read the new words to this old nursery rhyme, look for sixteen hidden objects in this silly scene. Find a frog, duck, apple, cat's head, seashell, heart, witch's head, dish, butterfly, cow, spoon, dog, toothbrush, rowboat, beetle, and a lizard.

113

Wake Up!

Time to rise and shine and search for hidden objects. Look for a mallet, crown, fork, artist's brush, wishbone, slice of pizza, carrot, teacup, ice-cream pop, jack-o'-lantern, spoon, pliers, and a candle.

Mary Cassatt

While the artist tries to paint a portrait, discover a shoe, tube of paint, egg, fish, carrot, fork, banana, caterpillar, feather, butterfly, snake, peacock, and a rabbit's head.

Ice-Cream Mouse

Here is a welcome sight on a hot day. Maybe he'll stop and help you find a mug, mitten, ice-cream pop, paintbrush, pencil, radish, magnifying glass, book, shovel, bicycle pump, toothbrush, and a shoe.

New Puppies

While Nicholas keeps an eye on these frisky puppies, cast your eye over the scene and find twenty hidden objects. Search for a heart, ring, butterfly, mushroom, saltshaker, book, rabbit, coffeepot, bird, horseshoe, hamburger, whale, eyeglasses, crescent moon, snake, pear, tepee, vase, banana, and a swan.

Fingerpainting

Melissa is so busy creating a masterpiece that she doesn't notice fourteen hidden objects around her. Can you find a bird, bell, ring, fish, lizard, toothbrush, light bulb, paper clip, pencil, spoon, banana, crescent moon, horn, and a sailboat?

118

Warm Weather Treats

The kids are enjoying cool drinks while Barney gets a cool bath. Can you find twenty-one hidden objects in this summertime scene? Look for a boomerang, cane, pennant, heart, flower, orange, seal, artist's brush, feather, crescent moon, sock, candle, mug, star, fish, pencil, carrot, eyeglasses, snake, tweezers, and a needle.

Ice-Skating Party

Peter, Penny, and Percy Penguin are having a good time. You can, too, by finding the hidden objects all around them. Look for a hockey stick, pliers, seal, light bulb, fish, carrot, dog bone, rabbit, sock, baseball cap, pear, moose's head, balloon, broom, and a canoe.

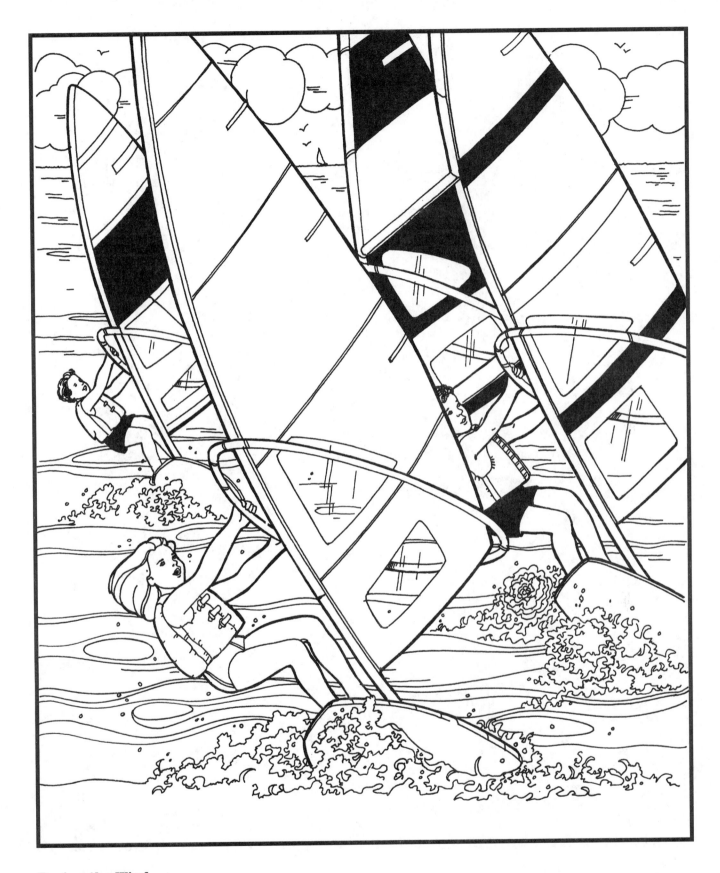

Racing the Wind

Who will reach the shoreline first? While you wait for the winner, search for a sneaker, carrot, fish, slice of pie, book, celery, sailboat, penguin, bird, apple, spoon, ice-cream cone, pennant, and a flower.

Fun on a Swing

While Buddy and Barry Bear take turns on the swing, see if you can find fourteen hidden objects. Look for a high-heeled shoe, sock, tack, spoon, caterpillar, lollipop, hockey stick, carrot, handbell, heart, needle, tulip, slice of pie, and a saucepan.

Bats from the Belfry

Before these critters fly home to their cave, find thirteen hidden objects in this nighttime scene. Search for a crown, eyeglasses, mitten, toothbrush, artist's brush, ruler, goose, pencil, saw, horn, sneaker, boomerang, and a banana.

Jungle Friends

Mowgli and Bagheera are enjoying the view from the treetops. Can you view seventeen hidden objects around them? Look for a bird, penguin, bell, heart, lizard, toothbrush, tweezers, turtle, mouse, goose, bowling pin, banana, paper clip, spoon, insect, sneaker, and a comb.

Clown School

Stop laughing at these silly clowns long enough to find a lollipop, slice of pizza, teacup and saucer, leaf, garlic, artist's brush, apple core, lampshade, sock, nail, shovel, banana, and an olive.

Look Out Below!

Will all the king's horsemen catch Humpty Dumpty if he falls? While Humpty tries to keep his balance, look for a spoon, sock, mug, shovel, mallet, baseball cap, open book, crown, scissors, caterpillar, paintbrush, moose's head, toothbrush, pencil, and a tack.

Say Cheese!

Will the photographer see the Bowser family or fourteen hidden objects? Can you see a kangaroo, lizard, pencil, rabbit, comb, screwdriver, open book, frog, nail, handbell, fan, hockey stick, squirrel, and a pennant?

The Best Tree

As the kids bring home their tree for Christmas, can you find twelve hidden objects in this snowy scene? Look for a mitten, frying pan, slice of pie, paintbrush, fountain pen, closed umbrella, spoon, saltshaker, pencil, candle, book, and a bell.

128

Water Volleyball

Here's a great game for a hot day. How many hidden objects can you find in this watery scene? Search for a cat, penguin, needle, chicken, snail, iron, flower, key, kangaroo, ladder, leaf, wishbone, and a safety pin.

The Animals Go Boating

It's a beautiful day to go boating, and this happy foursome is taking advantage of it. As they float down the stream, look for a spatula, cupcake, radish, bell, paintbrush, golf club, shoe, slice of cake,

pliers, carrot, key, artist's brush, slice of pie, ice-cream cone, whistle, pushpin, mug, safety pin, pencil, musical note, nail, mitten, spoon, open book, and a ballpoint pen.

Water from the Nile

While the Egyptian villagers fill their water jars, see if you can find fourteen hidden objects. Look for a slice of pie, worm, flashlight, wrapped present, scissors, needle, mushroom, flag, bowling pin, muffin, bird, toothbrush, fishhook, and a nail.

Sparrows

These happy songbirds are so busy gathering berries that they don't notice the twelve hidden objects around them. See if you can find a snake, boot, crayon, light bulb, seal, pocketknife, ant, shark, two dogs' heads, pencil, and a duck.

Yard Sale

How many objects are hiding among the bargains at this yard sale? Look for a broom, mushroom, slice of watermelon, ice-cream pop, eyeglasses, fish, teacup, ballpoint pen, tack, slice of pie, needle, musical note, and a sock.

Dog School

Are the students looking for answers or hidden objects? Help them find a knitted cap, flashlight, squirrel, fishhook, iron, hammer, hockey stick, boot, closed umbrella, shovel, baseball cap, pennant, tack, and a fork.

Poseidon

The god of the sea doesn't know that there are twelve hidden objects around him. Can you find a mouse, glove, banana, heart, goat's head, golf club, fish, sea gull, kangaroo, penguin, llama's head, and a weasel?

136

Alice at the Tea Party

While Alice tries to figure out what the Mad Hatter and the White Rabbit are talking about, see if you can spot a horn, handbell, bird, dog, shoe, banana, pencil, ring, deer, fish, butterfly, hammer, comb, and a snail.

Outer-Space Encounter

Have these little creatures come to search for hidden objects, too? Look for a shoe, spoon, pencil, trowel, elf's hat, ship, carrot, crown, snake, toothbrush, ladle, light bulb, and an ice-cream pop.

Take the Shot!

Will Marnie block Kayla's shot? While the girls try to even the score, see if you can find fifteen hidden objects in the gym. Search for a muffin, cat, mouse, penguin, eyeglasses, carrot, flute, horn, teacup, bowling pin, two birds, fish, toothbrush, and a ring.

Tree House Fun

Butch is not as eager as Smoky to be so far above the ground. Before they reach the tree house, see if you can find a snake, seal, sailboat, needle, eyeglasses, spoon, jar, pennant, fish, key, crescent moon, question mark, artist's brush, barbell, rabbit, and a cane.

Animals on Wheels

As these animal friends roll along together, look for twelve hidden objects in this country scene. Find a shoe, eyeglasses, key, fish, crayon, toothbrush, wrench, banana, screwdriver, candle, radish, and an artist's brush.

Springtime Stroll

What a fine day for a walk in the sunshine. How many hidden objects can you find among the animals and flowers? Search for a crescent moon, sock, oilcan, hatchet, tack, balloon, horse, acorn, pliers, spider, lollipop, artist's brush, and a ladle.

142

Wild Turkeys

What's hiding around these gobblers? Look for a fish, seal, mouse's head, mitten, mushroom, snake, heart, candle, rabbit's head, spoon, lizard, and a match.

Submarine

The diver in this little submarine can see some wonderful underwater sights. Can you see a hat, owl, bell, nail, sailboat, goose, ring, banana, eyeglasses, boomerang, flower, megaphone, teacup, and a glove?

144

Animals' Skating Party

What fun the animals are having on this wintry evening. While they skate together, see if you can find a pencil, fork, ant, shovel, crane, mouse, key, hairbrush, chicken, spoon, hammer, paper clip, bird, and a turtle.

Chasing Butterflies

Kitty is so busy trying to catch that butterfly that she doesn't see fifteen hidden objects all around her. See if you can find a duck, arrow, banana, bell, teapot, lion's head, crescent moon, hummingbird, bee, bat, trowel, fish, umbrella, rabbit, and a wishbone.

Art Class

What wonderful artwork will the children create today? Be creative and find fourteen hidden objects in the classroom. Look for a boot, banana, spool of thread, sheep, sock, fish, toothbrush, mug, tack, nail, comb, chicken, ice-cream cone, and a spoon.

Exploring the Moon

These astronauts have found all kinds of interesting things on the Moon's surface. See if you can locate a mitten, bell, spoon, lollipop, funnel, crayon, saucepan, eyeglasses, bird, pushpin, domino, key, magnifying glass, mug, dish, canoe paddle, ice-cream cone, button, whistle, hat, ring, wristwatch,

carrot, artist's brush, radish, mushroom, ladle, pencil, musical note, book, feather, fishhook, screw, worm, Christmas ornament, doughnut, and a shoe.

Scarecrow Show

Which scarecrow will win the prize? You'll win if you can find sixteen hidden objects in this scene. Look for a rabbit, mallet, spatula, shovel, fishhook, ice-cream cone, book, light bulb, tack, fish, paintbrush, slice of bread, ring, party hat, teacup, and a spoon.

150

To Banbury Cross

While the princess rides, see if you can find a lion cub, cane, dolphin, man's head, ant, snake, otter, boot, bird, envelope, toucan, fish, and a hammer.

Research at the Library

Will the kids find all the facts they need for their report? Will you find all the hidden objects? Look for a banana, shovel, paintbrush, crayon, slice of cake, slice of pie, mushroom, toothbrush, spatula, shoe, hammer, and a spoon.

Bunnies in the Garden

While the bunnies are busy harvesting their crops, see if you can dig up a potato, whale, shoehorn, chef's hat, hammer, needle, bird, duck, artist's brush, baseball glove, scissors, and a fish.

The Artist

This artist's favorite subject is himself! While he puts the finishing touches on his latest masterpiece, see if you can locate a mug, roller skate, slice of pie, umbrella, high-heeled shoe, birthday cake, mushroom, crown, baseball, telephone, butterfly, toothbrush, and a baseball bat.

Soup for Dinner

These little mice are so hungry for Mom's soup that they don't notice fourteen hidden objects around them. Look for a magnifying glass, ant, iron, strawberry, anchor, needle and thread, ring, arrow, duck, pennant, ice-cream cone, turtle, closed umbrella, and a fork.

Another Ringer!

Goat has found his mark today and is piling up the points. You can score some points by finding a dozen hidden objects in this scene. Find a flower, banana, spatula, slice of pie, rowboat, ice-cream cone, toothbrush, screwdriver, musical note, key, book, and a fishhook.

In the Jungle

Safari Sam is on the lookout for animals. You should be on the lookout for hidden objects. Discover a mug, pencil, comb, octopus, coffeepot, pair of pants, glove, dog, can, closed umbrella, scissors, and a fish.

Volleyball Action

Will Tim spike the ball and score another point? Will you find all the hidden objects here? Search for a cat, spatula, ladder, sneaker, pig, whale, nail, book, pitcher, hammer, rabbit, and a bird.

Winged Horses

While these mythical beasts soar above Atlantis, discover twelve hidden objects. Find a squirrel, book, lizard, fork, pennant, toothbrush, baseball cap, dog's head, arrowhead, butter knife, cat, and a hot dog.

Motorcycling Squirrels

As these two critters roar through the forest on their new motorcycle, search for twelve hidden objects. Find a golf club, wishbone, artist's brush, whistle, teacup, carrot, pushpin, spoon, cupcake, key, shoe, and a magnifying glass.

Rainy Day Stories

It's fun to read together on a cold, rainy day. While Megan reads to her sister, see if you can find a pencil, two cats, anteater, soda can, witch's hat, mug, paper clip, mushroom, duck, fish, ladybug, bottle, bird, and a banana.

Soccer in the Park

Tara tries to intercept the ball for her team, but Josh is too quick. How quickly can you discover a hammer, sailboat, cat, nail, pine tree, chick, ladle, saw, bird, bottle, fish, turtle, high-heeled shoe, seal, and a slice of pie?

Mini-Golf Fun

The kids are having so much fun playing miniature golf that they don't see fifteen objects hidden on the course. Look for a mallet, musical note, hammer, crescent moon, book, candle, carrot, fishhook, hanger, sock, tube of toothpaste, letter *E*, banana, artist's brush, and a trowel.

Breakdown on the Bridge

It looks as if Farmer Brown's truck has overheated. Stay cool while you search for a pencil, key, bell, tube of paint, mitten, shovel, shoe, screw, fish, mallet, ice-cream cone, and a magnifying glass.

Hippo Hygiene

Brushing three times a day keeps Hippo's teeth healthy and clean. You can clean up by finding fourteen hidden objects in the bathroom. Look for a turtle, iron, book, plunger, fishhook, pennant, duck tube, scissors, suitcase, dustpan, sailboat, ring, hanger, and a comb.

Hawaiian Dogs

While these clever canines learn to do the hula, search for sixteen hidden objects in this tropical scene. Find a canoe, banana, sock, wristwatch, spatula, bowl, apple core, dog bone, light bulb, butter knife, spool of thread, bell, book, ice-cream pop, pencil, and a flashlight.

Fishing on the Dock

Who will catch the biggest fish? See if you can fish for a paper clip, chair, television, clothespin, two birds, banana, sugar bowl, saucepan, snail, nail, toothbrush, hammer, fish, and a pencil.

ANSWERS

Cover: banana, hairbrush, screwdriver, teacup, spoon, mushroom, watering can, bowl, book, ice-cream cone, toothbrush, domino, wishbone

3: ring, banana, tube of toothpaste, rabbit, pencil, butter knife, shovel, slice of pie, baseball bat, horseshoe, sailboat, slice of bread, wristwatch

4: bird, stork, two kangaroos, iron, key, two cats, bell, guitar, rabbit, teacup, sock, belt, sea gull

5: ghost, sock, bell, wedge of cheese, pear, crescent moon, telescope, heart, mushroom, tack, penguin, paintbrush, lollipop, ladle, mug, turtle, broccoli, ring, sailboat, ax, crayon, cupcake, ice-cream pop, bat

6: turtle, baseball bat, saltshaker, pumpkin, fish, boomerang, bowling ball, envelope, snake, hairbrush, tube of paint, mushroom, needle, book

7: fishhook, teacup, slipper, hat, banana, bell, toothbrush, worm, hockey stick, candy, slice of watermelon, spoon

168

8-9: duck, scarf, clarinet, yo-yo, balloon, hoe, grasshopper, butterfly, safety pin, bell, coffeepot, envelope, fish, trowel, saw, cupcake, belt, hammer, crescent moon, key, snake, snail, eyeglasses, frog, candy cane, hockey stick, fishhook, ring, bottle, ladle, comb

10: hat, artist's brush, fish, tweezers, scissors, bowling ball, safety pin, bird, bell, acorn, cherries, bee, needle, banana

11: candle, slice of cake, needle, key, sneaker, paintbrush, slice of pie, bell, spoon, cupcake, pushpin, wishbone

12: pennant, worm, hoe, lollipop, wooden shoe, banana, golf club, drumstick, slice of cake, top hat, fish, paintbrush

13: hat, pencil, egg, toothbrush, carrot, spoon, saw, duck, horn, bell, tweezers, paper clip, fish

14: kite, duck, pennant, fish, top hat, horn, sailboat, hammer, gopher, ice-cream cone, baseball bat, frog, banana

15: broom, sock, trowel, crescent moon, candle, cat, shoe, witch's hat, fire hydrant, frying pan, pliers, baby's bottle, toothbrush, bird, book

16: fish, open book, comb, lollipop, crescent moon, slice of watermelon, toothbrush, tack, ladle, teacup, banana, pencil

17: comb, fish, shoe, fishhook, rabbit, snake, cat, glove, heart, slice of bread, paper clip, pitchfork, spoon

18: whistle, rabbit, rolling pin, crown, glove, hammer, teacup, dolphin, wristwatch, cupcake, hat, handbell, butterfly

19: rabbit, mouse, banana, pennant, frying pan, bowl, saltshaker, shovel, needle, bird, hairbrush, fishing pole, squirrel

20: spatula, eyeglasses, fish, artist's brush, bicycle pump, pencil, mallet, crayon, pushpin, safety pin, spoon, musical note

21: chair, hairbrush, tepee, shark, C-clamp, pencil, ax, screwdriver, mug of coffee, teddy bear, book, bird, toolbox, light bulb

24: pencil, slice of pie, screwdriver, nail, ice-cream pop, toothbrush, lollipop, shoe, envelope, boot, kite, handbell, candle

25: seal, pennant, duck, mouse, suitcase, stork, dragonfly, sailboat, scissors, hairbrush, fork, insect, bow tie, spoon

26: book, pencil, heart, dog, flag, paintbrush, candle, sneaker, light bulb, caterpillar, snail, chicken, banana

27: shoe, pear, cookie, nail, hair dryer, ruler, penguin, pitcher, elephant, ladle, ear of corn, hat, straight pin, ice scraper, banana

28: squirrel, broom, sock, baseball bat, seal, hammer, fan, snail, key, canoe, thimble, butterfly, mushroom, pencil, high-heeled boot, handbell

29: key, banana, book, eyeglasses, fish, ring, megaphone, ladder, hanger, pair of pants, eagle's head, paper clip, comb, duck

30: rabbit, saltshaker, fish, trowel, slice of pizza, spoon, pencil, sock, crescent moon, open book, hammer, bird

31: carrot, book, mitten, pushpin, spatula, radish, wishbone, nail, slice of pie, ice-cream cone, candle, hoe

32: ring, comb, drinking straw, snake, boot, hat, telephone receiver, artist's brush, fishhook, golf club, tack, eyeglasses, banana

33: mouse, flashlight, sock, magnifying glass, fish, hairbrush, frog, anchor, pitcher, rabbit, light bulb, carrot, lizard, candle

34: open book, sock, tube of toothpaste, ax, flowerpot, baseball cap, butterfly, mug, apple, banana, slice of bread, ice-cream cone, bell, wishbone, mouse, mushroom, mallet, cupcake, magnifying glass, pennant, pitcher, egg, pencil, saucepan, needle

35: cane, bell, alligator, dinosaur, pencil, iron, paintbrush, fish, soda can, balloon, paper airplane, bottle, toothbrush, computer screen, two dogs' heads

36-37: boot, spoon, safety pin, frying pan, ice-cream cone, flag, teacup, book, toothbrush, fish, ring, comb, heart, duck, hat, T-shirt, gingerbread man, cat, tweezers, kite, crown, tack, glove, bell, paper clip, pitchfork

38: saltshaker, crayon, scissors, open book, knitted cap, spoon, mushroom, shovel, rabbit, worm, seal, sneaker, cupcake

39: pear, eyeglasses, wooden shoe, rowboat, teacup, spool of thread, penguin, fishhook, brick, peanut, banana, baseball bat, feather

40: top hat, rooster, mouse's head, hand mirror, bow tie, artist's brush, ax, hourglass, slice of bread, butter knife, ice-cream cone, needle, knitted cap

41: mitten, spoon, ice-cream cone, lollipop, slice of pie, turtle, question mark, pennant, crayon, knitted cap, snake, slice of cake, mushroom, fish, artist's brush, tube of toothpaste, sailboat, bell, bird, birdhouse, tack, trowel, open book, drinking glass

42: cherry, acorn, mouse, carrot, turtle, chicken, rabbit's head, teacup, snail, bee, bird, crab, number 7, paper clip, needle, fish

43: mug, shovel, pliers, radish, toothbrush, ballpoint pen, nail, fish, spoon, artist's brush, musical note, eyeglasses, fishhook

44: snail, plate, ruler, rabbit, seal, sailboat, toothbrush, butterfly, dog, dolphin, mouse, paper clip, teacup, key, fish, banana

45: bowl, seal, cat, golf club, baseball cap, sailboat, worm, teapot, banana, fish, pitcher, carrot, teacup

46-47: snake, handbell, horn, closed umbrella, horseshoe, ladle, dragonfly, bowl, flaming torch, trowel, fork, scissors, crown, boomerang, flag, cane, cherry, pencil, button, light bulb, needle, fish, crescent moon, ice-cream cone, yo-yo

48: baseball cap, teacup, horn, ice-cream cone, toothbrush, fish, needle, banana, crown, flag, feather, heart, paper clip, slipper, pencil

49: paper clip, pennant, dragonfly, high-heeled shoe, bow tie, iron, mug, telephone receiver, bird, key, saw, elf's hat, spoon, centipede

50: bowl, crescent moon, slice of pizza, teacup, banana, butterfly, slice of lemon, toothbrush, apple core, spoon, fork, artist's brush

51: cupcake, crown, baseball cap, goose, hatchet, toothbrush, fish, ladder, ice-cream cone, carrot, butterfly, ice-cream pop, handbell, artist's brush, pencil

52: heart, pennant, ice-cream cone, sheep, fish, hand mirror, trowel, letter *V*, cane, ladder, letter *U*, bee, arrow, letter *L*, letter *F*, cat's head, artist's brush, bird

53: bird, dinosaur, banana, sailboat, ladder, ice-cream pop, heart, baseball bat, shoe, comb, pennant, football, mitten

54: tack, banana, jack-o'-lantern, bird, worm, baseball, ram's head, hot-air balloon, deer's head, duck, telescope, ruler, insect, battery

55: saw, top hat, eagle's head, plate, glove, pencil, hammer, flag, megaphone, alligator, nail, artist's brush, fish, crown

56: sailboat, bird, mushroom, crescent moon, question mark, tepee, fish, pitchfork, needle, cat, lollipop, pliers, banana, umbrella, rabbit's head, tack

57: drumstick, apple, sock, mitten, bell, dog, elf, heart, elf's hat, ice skate, candle, squirrel, slice of cake, snowmobile, ice-cream cone, crayon, knitted cap

58-59: shovel, tack, arrow, rabbit's head, crescent moon, teacup, spatula, trowel, envelope, pickax, telephone pole, sailboat, eyeglasses, ladle, fish, mushroom, chicken, hanger, hoe, stork's head, banana, slice of pizza, fishing pole, candle, boomerang, ladder, needle, frying pan, closed umbrella, domino

60: chair, doll, bottle, boot, hourglass, fan, octopus, pacifier, fish, horse, jester's head, banana

61: sheep, mushroom, wedge of cheese, artist's brush, starfish, dog bone, radish, three arrows, slice of pie, hedgehog, slice of bread, worm

62: pennant, spoon, key, portable radio, rabbit, ice-cream cone, saltshaker, fish, slice of pie, bat, pear, artist's brush, knitted cap, tack, lollipop

63: feather, mitten, cat, sheep, dog bone, spoon, sock, sailboat, rowboat, pencil, potato, bear, hanger

64: pie, baseball bat, turtle, cat, glove, three birds, potato, high-heeled shoe, butterfly, pliers, rabbit, candle, wishbone, mouse, bear cub, wristwatch

65: whistle, magnifying glass, toothbrush, hammer, feather, bell, pencil, fish, hoe, chair, paintbrush, closed umbrella

66: hairbrush, sock, tree, ax, sailboat, mushroom, ice-cream cone, strawberry, carrot, bird, acorn, pencil

67: ring, pail, light bulb, plunger, toothbrush, mallet, closed umbrella, mug, penguin, fishhook, duck, fork, pencil

68: book, dog bone, penguin, Santa's hat, ice-cream pop, wishbone, fork, apple core, light bulb, artist's brush, bird, mouse, pencil, spoon

69: flashlight, loaf of bread, hammer, bird, binoculars, letter *C*, nail, kite, pitcher, clarinet, violin bow, cat's head, hockey stick, hat

70-71: dragon's head, sock, slice of pie, leaf, spoon, whale, two fish, seal, closed umbrella, two rabbits, rooster, ballpoint pen, chick, dandelion, artist's brush, squirrel, ladder, feather, slice of bread, goose, owl, three birds, elf's head, shoe, cat, mouse, milking stool, feather duster, needle, zipper, saucepan, crescent moon, lizard, carrot, dog, light bulb

72: bird, comb, heart, mouse, nail, fish, goose, snake, elf's hat, crescent moon, spoon, fork, hammer

73: feather, candle, wishbone, hammer, recorder, shovel, magnifying glass, carrot, closed umbrella, clothespin, paintbrush, mug

74: baseball cap, comb, three birds, pennant, elf's hat, horn, car, saw, spoon, closed umbrella, nail, key

75: hammer, comb, carrot, fork, party hat, book, baseball cap, bird, hat, fish, banana, witch's hat, tack

76: bowling pin, tack, sock, teacup, handbell, candle, key, duck, fish, sneaker, snake, crescent moon

77: cupcake, ice-cream cone, dog's head, jump rope, pencil, slice of bread, paper airplane, soda can, rabbit, iron, hairbrush, orange, bell, artist's brush

78: feather, open book, sailboat, heart, spoon, fish, teacup, baseball cap, horn, ladder, straight pin, kite, crown, dog, mouse

79: flashlight, hummingbird, whistle, light bulb, pear, radish, teacup, safety pin, bell, book, spoon, ice-cream pop, feather, hairbrush, flower, toothbrush

80-81: candle, spatula, ballpoint pen, slice of cake, book, wrench, teacup, screw, slice of pie, padlock, crayon, ice-cream pop, whistle, key, mushroom, pencil, celery, cupcake, mallet, flower, ladle, golf club, artist's brush, shovel, toothbrush

82: screw, broom, baseball bat, artist's brush, two birds, pig, carrot, ladder, knitted cap, rabbit, telephone receiver, funnel, nail, butter knife, fish, chess pawn, spoon

179

83: fork, mallet, spoon, shark, fishhook, sock, glove, comb, rabbit, ring, butter knife, needle, nail

84: pumpkin, snake, toothbrush, teacup, pencil, pliers, ring, sailboat, key, fish, coffeepot, airplane, mushroom, boot, bird

85: ring, rabbit, spoon, bird, eyeglasses, needle, hammer, scissors, whistle, butterfly, ice-cream cone, artist's brush

86: ring, banana, fish, crescent moon, glove, crown, fishhook, heart, horn, straight pin, ruler, paper clip, toothbrush, teacup

87: mitten, pliers, comb, safety pin, half an apple, book, shoe, paintbrush, pushpin, cupcake, feather, hoe, trowel, bell, radish, pencil

88: sock, iron, loaf of bread, clothespin, wristwatch, slice of cake, cat, flashlight, teacup, knitted cap, owl, baby's rattle, telephone receiver, pencil

89: shovel, seal, slice of cake, arrow, needle, book, carrot, wishbone, toothbrush, candle, ice-cream cone, ice scraper, golf club

90: banana, toothbrush, artist's brush, feather, pear, bird, boomerang, sailboat, slice of pie, kite, flowerpot, fork

91: dolphin, pig, heart, rhinoceros, turtle, sea horse, koala bear, bear's head, frog, lady's head, butterfly, candy cane, bird

92: glove, baseball bat, sailboat, mouse, spoon, butter knife, belt, candle, mallet, bird, witch's hat, cane, seal

93: lollipop, hatchet, mushroom, goblet, ring, sailboat, arrow, yo-yo, balloon, snake, top, needle, funnel, candle

94: slice of bread, recorder, bell, carrot, butter knife, scrub brush, flashlight, mallet, half an apple, crayon, fountain pen, shoe

95: carrot, sneaker, rabbit, lollipop, golf club, mug, snake, ice-cream cone, sheep, spoon, duck, cane, glove, telephone receiver

96: belt, iron, squirrel, teacup, fishhook, key, pennant, hammer, spoon, toothbrush, car, pencil, horn, handbell

97: horn, ring, needle, pencil, toothbrush, open book, glove, fish, bell, kite, comb, sock, saw

98: slice of watermelon, saltshaker, banana, sock, balloon, shoe, fork, crescent moon, bowling pin, magnet, doll, butterfly, vase, bowl, spoon, bird, comb

99: pennant, pencil, duck, glove, chicken, ice-cream cone, sailboat, eyeglasses, saw, crescent moon, crown, camel, banana

100: worm, golf club, tack, shoe, sock, heart, crown, cupcake, pencil, spoon, hammer, number 8, ring, drumstick

101: squirrel, hammer, handbell, screwdriver, rabbit, flashlight, artist's brush, slipper, frog, pencil, toothbrush, duck, penguin

102: pitcher, rabbit, turtle, poodle, sock, cat, goose, spoon, kite, mouse, sea gull, paintbrush, bat, iron

103: sailboat, fish, two eggs, eyeglasses, saw, toothbrush, banana, comb, crescent moon, stick of gum, roller skate, heart, mug

104-105: book, feather, nail, carrot, grapes, mallet, hammer, butter knife, key, crayon, fountain pen, spoon, celery, toothbrush, slice of pie, candle, pencil, bell, mitten, screwdriver, apple core, slice of cake, artist's brush, radish, razor

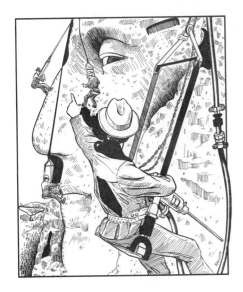

106: pencil, pie, paintbrush, spoon, comb, horseshoe, golf club, pushpin, gravy boat, needle, elf's shoe, sock, squirrel, tape dispenser, hanger

107: rhinoceros, fish, eagle's head, ice-cream cone, bell, paper clip, rocking horse, crown, open book, saw, toothbrush, heart, banana, teacup, glove

108: Goofus, Gallant, Tommy Timbertoe, Spot, Aloysius the Wolf, Poozy Bear, closed umbrella, artist's brush, bee, ladle, apple, butterfly, baseball bat, star, needle, banana, necktie, candle, bird's head, eyeglasses, pennant, insect, pencil

109: pencil, banana, dog, shovel, eyeglasses, handbell, fish, paper clip, wild turkey, heart, toothbrush, sailboat, ice-cream cone

110: mop, toothbrush, milking stool, spoon, teacup, boot, open book, bell, hat, lollipop, balloon, crescent moon, hammer

111: golf club, screw, magnifying glass, slice of cake, spoon, mallet, ice-cream cone, tube of toothpaste, bell, artist's brush, book, pencil

112: flashlight, light bulb, sailboat, ice-cream cone, two hearts, spoon, doughnut, toothbrush, dog, horn, banana, duck, book, pencil

113: frog, duck, apple, cat's head, seashell, heart, witch's head, dish, butterfly, cow, spoon, dog, toothbrush, rowboat, beetle, lizard

114: mallet, crown, fork, artist's brush, wishbone, slice of pizza, carrot, teacup, ice-cream pop, jack-o'-lantern, spoon, pliers, candle

115: shoe, tube of paint, egg, fish, carrot, fork, banana, caterpillar, feather, butterfly, snake, peacock, rabbit's head

116: mug, mitten, ice-cream pop, paintbrush, pencil, radish, magnifying glass, book, shovel, bicycle pump, toothbrush, shoe

117: heart, ring, butterfly, mushroom, saltshaker, book, rabbit, coffeepot, bird, horseshoe, hamburger, whale, eyeglasses, crescent moon, snake, pear, tepee, vase, banana, swan

118: bird, bell, ring, fish, lizard, toothbrush, light bulb, paper clip, pencil, spoon, banana, crescent moon, horn, sailboat

119: boomerang, cane, pennant, heart, flower, orange, seal, artist's brush, feather, crescent moon, sock, candle, mug, star, fish, pencil, carrot, eyeglasses, snake, tweezers, needle

120: hockey stick, pliers, seal, light bulb, fish, carrot, dog bone, rabbit, sock, baseball cap, pear, moose's head, balloon, broom, canoe

121: sneaker, carrot, fish, slice of pie, book, celery, sailboat, penguin, bird, apple, spoon, ice-cream cone, pennant, flower

122: high-heeled shoe, sock, tack, spoon, caterpillar, lollipop, hockey stick, carrot, handbell, heart, needle, tulip, slice of pie, saucepan

123: crown, eyeglasses, mitten, toothbrush, artist's brush, ruler, goose, pencil, saw, horn, sneaker, boomerang, banana

124: bird, penguin, bell, heart, lizard, toothbrush, tweezers, turtle, mouse, goose, bowling pin, banana, paper clip, spoon, insect, sneaker, comb

125: lollipop, slice of pizza, teacup and saucer, leaf, garlic, artist's brush, apple core, lampshade, sock, nail, shovel, banana, olive

126: spoon, sock, mug, shovel, mallet, baseball cap, open book, crown, scissors, caterpillar, paintbrush, moose's head, toothbrush, pencil, tack

127: kangaroo, lizard, pencil, rabbit, comb, screwdriver, open book, frog, nail, handbell, fan, hockey stick, squirrel, pennant

128: mitten, frying pan, slice of pie, paintbrush, fountain pen, closed umbrella, spoon, saltshaker, pencil, candle, book, bell

129: cat, penguin, needle, chicken, snail, iron, flower, key, kangaroo, ladder, leaf, wishbone, safety pin

130-131: spatula, cupcake, radish, bell, paintbrush, golf club, shoe, slice of cake, pliers, carrot, key, artist's brush, slice of pie, ice-cream cone, whistle, pushpin, mug, safety pin, pencil, musical note, nail, mitten, spoon, open book, ballpoint pen

132: slice of pie, worm, flashlight, wrapped present, scissors, needle, mushroom, flag, bowling pin, muffin, bird, toothbrush, fishhook, nail

133: snake, boot, crayon, light bulb, seal, pocketknife, ant, shark, two dogs' heads, pencil, duck

134: broom, mushroom, slice of watermelon, ice-cream pop, eyeglasses, fish, teacup, ballpoint pen, tack, slice of pie, needle, musical note, sock

135: knitted cap, flashlight, squirrel, fishhook, iron, hammer, hockey stick, boot, closed umbrella, shovel, baseball cap, pennant, tack, fork

136: mouse, glove, banana, heart, goat's head, golf club, fish, sea gull, kangaroo, penguin, llama's head, weasel

137: horn, handbell, bird, dog, shoe, banana, pencil, ring, deer, fish, butterfly, hammer, comb, snail

138: shoe, spoon, pencil, trowel, elf's hat, ship, carrot, crown, snake, toothbrush, ladle, light bulb, ice-cream pop

139: muffin, cat, mouse, penguin, eyeglasses, carrot, flute, horn, teacup, bowling pin, two birds, fish, toothbrush, ring

140: snake, seal, sailboat, needle, eyeglasses, spoon, jar, pennant, fish, key, crescent moon, question mark, artist's brush, barbell, rabbit, cane

141: shoe, eyeglasses, key, fish, crayon, toothbrush, wrench, banana, screwdriver, candle, radish, artist's brush

142: crescent moon, sock, oilcan, hatchet, tack, balloon, horse, acorn, pliers, spider, lollipop, artist's brush, ladle

143: fish, seal, mouse's head, mitten, mushroom, snake, heart, candle, rabbit's head, spoon, lizard, match

144: hat, owl, bell, nail, sailboat, goose, ring, banana, eyeglasses, boomerang, flower, megaphone, teacup, glove

145: pencil, fork, ant, shovel, crane, mouse, key, hairbrush, chicken, spoon, hammer, paper clip, bird, turtle

146: duck, arrow, banana, bell, teapot, lion's head, crescent moon, hummingbird, bee, bat, trowel, fish, umbrella, rabbit, wishbone

147: boot, banana, spool of thread, sheep, sock, fish, toothbrush, mug, tack, nail, comb, chicken, ice-cream cone, spoon

148-149: mitten, bell, spoon, lollipop, funnel, crayon, saucepan, eyeglasses, bird, pushpin, domino, key, magnifying glass, mug, dish, canoe paddle, ice-cream cone, button, whistle, hat, ring, wristwatch, carrot, artist's brush, radish, mushroom, ladle, pencil, musical note, book, feather, fishhook, screw, worm, Christmas ornament, doughnut, shoe

150: rabbit, mallet, spatula, shovel, fishhook, ice-cream cone, book, light bulb, tack, fish, paintbrush, slice of bread, ring, party hat, teacup, spoon

151: lion cub, cane, dolphin, man's head, ant, snake, otter, boot, bird, envelope, toucan, fish, hammer

152: banana, shovel, paintbrush, crayon, slice of cake, slice of pie, mushroom, toothbrush, spatula, shoe, hammer, spoon

153: potato, whale, shoehorn, chef's hat, hammer, needle, bird, duck, artist's brush, baseball glove, scissors, fish

154: mug, roller skate, slice of pie, umbrella, high-heeled shoe, birthday cake, mushroom, crown, baseball, telephone, butterfly, toothbrush, baseball bat

155: magnifying glass, ant, iron, strawberry, anchor, needle and thread, ring, arrow, duck, pennant, ice-cream cone, turtle, closed umbrella, fork

156: flower, banana, spatula, slice of pie, rowboat, ice-cream cone, toothbrush, screwdriver, musical note, key, book, fishhook

157: mug, pencil, comb, octopus, coffeepot, pair of pants, glove, dog, can, closed umbrella, scissors, fish

158: cat, spatula, ladder, sneaker, pig, whale, nail, book, pitcher, hammer, rabbit, bird

159: squirrel, book, lizard, fork, pennant, toothbrush, baseball cap, dog's head, arrowhead, butter knife, cat, hot dog

160: golf club, wishbone, artist's brush, whistle, teacup, carrot, pushpin, spoon, cupcake, key, shoe, magnifying glass

161: pencil, two cats, anteater, soda can, witch's hat, mug, paper clip, mushroom, duck, fish, ladybug, bottle, bird, banana

162: hammer, sailboat, cat, nail, pine tree, chick, ladle, saw, bird, bottle, fish, turtle, high-heeled shoe, seal, slice of pie

163: mallet, musical note, hammer, crescent moon, book, candle, carrot, fishhook, hanger, sock, tube of toothpaste, letter *E*, banana, artist's brush, trowel

164: pencil, key, bell, tube of paint, mitten, shovel, shoe, screw, fish, mallet, ice-cream cone, magnifying glass

165: turtle, iron, book, plunger, fishhook, pennant, duck tube, scissors, suitcase, dustpan, sailboat, ring, hanger, comb

166: canoe, banana, sock, wristwatch, spatula, bowl, apple core, dog bone, light bulb, butter knife, spool of thread, bell, book, ice-cream pop, pencil, flashlight

167: paper clip, chair, television, clothespin, two birds, banana, sugar bowl, saucepan, snail, nail, toothbrush, hammer, fish, pencil